INTRODUCTION BY ALAN BISBORT

Compiled and Edited by Allen Boyce Eddington

POMEGRANATE ARTBOOKS • SAN FRANCISCO

Published by Pomegranate Artbooks
Box 6099, Rohnert Park, California 94927

Pomegranate Europe Ltd.
Fullbridge House, Fullbridge
Maldon, Essex CM9 7LE, England

Library of Congress Cataloging-in-Publication Data

Einstein, Albert, 1879–1955.
    Essential Einstein / introduction by Alan Bisbort. — 1st ed.
        p.   cm.
    ISBN 0-87654-472-3
    1. Einstein, Albert, 1879–1955—Pictorial works. I. Bisbort,
Alan, 1953–   . II. Title.
QC16.E5E392 1995
530´.092—dc20   95-30369
                                         CIP

Pomegranate Catalog No. A800

Designed by Bonnie Smetts Design

Printed in Korea
00 99 98 97 96 95   6 5 4 3 2 1

First Edition

INTRODUCTION

BY ALAN BISBORT

A BLOCK FROM THE MALL IN WASHINGTON, D.C. —just off the beaten path of most tourists—is a bronze statue of Albert Einstein (American, 1879–1955) that perhaps says more about the man than the sculptor intended. Hidden in an unmarked park on the Constitution Avenue side of the National Academy of Sciences and protected by a canopy of elm trees and holly bushes, the statue is as inconspicuous as any seven-thousand-pound, twelve-foot-tall monument can be.

In such a tranquil setting, favored more by birds and squirrels than by people, Einstein—despite his larger-than-life size— seems as approachable as a beloved old uncle spinning a bedtime yarn. In fact, the man who peeled back the outer layer of the universe and revealed secrets more powerful than our wildest imaginings seems ready for his own night's repose. Slumped on a bronze bench, eyes half-closed, Einstein leans to one side, as if exhausted from a day's labors. The overwhelming impulse of visitors is to climb onto the bench and curl up in this gentle man's lap, pat his iconically famous mane of hair, and pose for the obligatory snapshot.

Glimpsed hurriedly through a break in the foliage, say, from a moving vehicle on the avenue, Einstein as he's portrayed in this placid shrine might be mistaken for a homeless person who has found a temporary haven. The statue, in this respect, is not an inappropriate metaphor for the man. Very much at home in the nation's capital, with the ear of the president, and welcomed with open arms to these shores in 1933 when he moved to Princeton to head the new Institute for Advanced Study, Einstein was compelled by conscience to renounce his German citizenship (on two separate occasions) and eventually became a citizen of Switzerland and the United States. He was an internationalist in outlook, a pacifist by nature, and a humanitarian at heart. In short, Einstein was more at home in the universe than behind the borders of any nation-state.

Like Einstein's life story and his life's work in physics, the path to his statue can't be seen at first glance or described in one sentence. An American journalist once asked the great physicist for a one-sentence definition of his relativity theory. Einstein responded—earnestly and without rancor— that it would require three days for a short definition, and then paused, as if waiting for the journalist to begin taking notes. At once playful and serious, complex and eminently simple, Einstein was more than

the sum of his portraits—including this loving tribute to him outside the National Academy of Sciences.

Should a visitor look a bit more closely at this Einstein shrine, perhaps even wander into the seldom-visited Academy, a glimmer of the man's complexity might begin to emerge. For example, that bronze tablet in his hands—the one most tourists lean against to steady themselves for their souvenir snapshot—has inscribed upon it the simple but terribly momentous formula for which Einstein the physicist is best known: $E = mc^2$. A formula everyone knows but few truly understand. Another not inappropriate metaphor for the man whose profound impact on science and humanity almost beggars the imagination—and thus begs to be reduced in order to be comprehended.

Or, how about the circular sky map—into the face of which are pounded 2,700 metal studs—that surrounds the statue? Nothing simple about that. The studs represent the sun, planets, moons, and stars that are visible to the naked eye. This is the same visible universe that baffled, amazed, and terrified human beings for 15,000 years before Sir Isaac Newton calmed the waters of the Enlightenment with his seemingly unshakable theory of how it all fit so neatly together. Only 200 years later, however, along came Albert Einstein, whose special relativity theory of 1905 and general theory of relativity in 1916 upset Newton's apple cart, erased his blackboard, and drew upon it an entirely new concept of our universe. "A new figure in world history," proclaimed the *Berliner Illustrirte Zeitung* on December 14, 1919, beneath a picture of Einstein, "whose investigations signify a complete revision of our concepts of nature."

No wonder this kindly man came to represent the stereotype of the absent-minded professor, the inscrutable but trustworthy holder of profound secrets. "The Einstein we can all understand," says the author of the introduction to Einstein's *The World As I See It* (1930), "is no less great than the Einstein we take on trust." Certainly, we trust this Einstein we see outside the National Academy of Sciences, though most of us will never be able to approach his science with any ease. We know that his theory of relativity made possible the eventual unlocking of the atom, for good and ill. We also know that his work on behalf of humanity can never be measured in a mathematical formula or a single explosive experiment.

Thus the statue we see is as enigmatic, and as complex, as the man. It sits across the Mall from the memorial to Abraham Lincoln, another complex man who profoundly altered history but is often reduced to his simplest parts. Closer still is the Vietnam Veterans Memorial, a sunken meditation chamber across the street from Einstein, where grown men often weep openly, unabashedly, trying to understand the sadness of war and violence. Look closely at Einstein's statue and you will see the sadness there too, a humanizing emotion for someone whose professional work was beyond the ability of most humans to understand.

Still, among these three very American memorials, a visitor to Washington, D.C., can't help but feel most comforted in the green space surrounding Einstein's statue. Sphinxlike but approachable, off the beaten path but not dangerously removed, he both comforts and confounds us, a Zen koan in bronze.

■ ■ ■ ■ ■ ■ ■

Another great American is called to mind by this image of Einstein in Washington, D.C.—Walt Whitman, the poet who celebrated both the individual and the universal and became the "sage of Camden." Though he was often misunderstood or taken on faith by his admirers, Whitman also became a much-coveted oracle of wisdom and humanitarianism. The many wonderful portraits and photographs of Walt Whitman, especially those taken of him late in his life, suggest a public persona and a private humaneness not unlike Einstein's, so obvious and consistent in the portrait of him presented on these pages in pictures and words.

Both of these men spent their lives affirming things, not negating them. Both experienced the horrors of war but emerged without bitterness or hopelessness. They both preached the interdependence—the relativity—of all things. "For every atom belonging to me," wrote Whitman in "Song of Myself," "as good belongs to you." They both believed in what Whitman called "the common air that bathes the globe." They both were deep theoretical thinkers, visionaries. "I am afoot with my vision," exulted Whitman; "Space and Time, now I see it is true, what I guessed at as I walked the beach under the paling stars of the morning."

Is this really so far removed from what Einstein must have felt when he glanced at the heavens? After all, as Anthony Storr points out in *The Dynamics of Creation*, "the most remarkable thing about Einstein's achievements is that his discoveries were made almost entirely by thought alone, unsupported at first by much experiment, or indeed by much mathematics. . . . He had absolute faith in his own insight."

Both were deeply spiritual individuals, yet neither had a concept of God that would pass muster in an organized world religion. "I have no chair, no church, no philosophy," Whitman claimed, and Einstein echoed with "In this materialistic age of ours the serious scientific workers are the only profoundly religious people."

Perhaps the most appropriate similarity between these two great men can be found in Whitman's famous lines at the end of "Song of Myself": "Do I contradict myself? / Very well then I contradict myself, / (I am large, I contain multitudes)."

■ ■ ■ ■ ■ ■ ■

The contradictions of this multitude we call Albert Einstein began early in his life. Born in Swabia, he grew up in Germany but at age sixteen renounced his German citizenship to become Swiss. As a boy, he was not a particularly good or disciplined student. He did, however, display a facility for mathematics and philosophy, and by fourteen he had surpassed his masters. Instead of occupying himself in a manner befitting a teenager, Einstein could be heard to ask questions like "What would the world look like if I rode on a beam of light?"

Although much of this was due to his visionary nature, part of it was pure and simple rebellion against his authoritarian German schoolmasters. It was, in fact, only after he enrolled at the Aargau Canton School in Aargau and the Swiss Federal Polytechnic School in Zurich that Einstein began to bloom as a student. He found the democratic and pacifist spirit of Zurich so much more to his liking than the militarism of his old hometown, Munich, that he renounced his German citizenship for the first time then, an amazing act for a

teenager. He stayed in Switzerland for several years, yet still he drifted in the clouds of scientific theory.

Even during the greatest flowering of his theoretical physics, Einstein was not affiliated with any outstanding institution—he was, in fact, a patent examiner at the customs office in Berne, a seven-year stint that he considered the happiest period of his life. This idyll ended when he issued his special relativity theory in 1905, accepted an appointment as a lecturer at the University of Bern in 1908, and resigned from the patent office and accepted an associate professorship at the University of Zurich the following year. In 1913 he accepted another professorship in Berlin, at the newly formed Institute of Physics. He regained his German citizenship then but retained his Swiss citizenship.

Einstein's chosen work was immersed in the world's longest-running contradiction—that which exists between science and religion. He never doubted that his work in relativity would reconcile these two disparate entities. The religious feeling of the scientist, he wrote, "takes the form of a rapturous amazement at the harmony of natural law, which reveals an intelligence of such superiority that, compared with it, all the systematic thinking and acting of human beings is an utterly insignificant reflection." An unorthodox religious view, surely, but one that seems acceptable in

today's world. At the time, though, Einstein was castigated by fundamentalists of all stripes. The Vatican treated him only a little less harshly than it did Galileo, accusing Einstein of "authentic atheism even if it is camouflaged as cosmic pantheism."

This was in addition to the backlash against Einstein from some of his fellow German citizens, who—guided by the nascent and rancid tremors of the rising Nazi Party—dubbed his work "Jewish science" and "the Einstein hoax." He received hate mail. His family and co-workers were threatened. One man offered a reward for anyone who would assassinate Einstein—and was fined all of sixteen dollars. And yet, through these slights and threats Einstein persevered, stoic on the outside, bubbling with indignation on the inside. In all but two years between 1910 and 1921 he was nominated for the Nobel Prize in physics, finally winning it in 1921, bringing undeserved acclaim to his temporarily adopted country.

The notoriety that attended the Nobel allowed Einstein to express his political feelings openly, which calls up another contradiction, that between his ease of fellowship with other people and his profound love of—and need for—solitude. "I live in that solitude which is painful in youth," he wrote in 1936, "but delicious in maturity." This perhaps explains the rumpled appearance for which he seems most remembered—the baggy trousers, smoldering pipe, unkempt hair, old sweaters. Jacob Bronowski, in *The Ascent of Man*, tells of how he, as a young student, sat in on an Einstein lecture. The world-renowned professor tottered into class in a frayed sweater and slippers with no socks, as if he'd just gotten out of bed, which, of course, he had not. This was simply how he dressed all the time, at home and in the world. "Plain living is good for everybody, physically and mentally," he said.

Einstein's personality also contained multitudes. To reporters he was often ironic but not openly hostile. To leaders and dignitaries he was self-effacing but proud, dignified but bemused (after sitting through several formal occasions, he wrote to his wife that he'd conceived of "a new theory of eternity"). He could be cranky and even despairing, lashing out at contemporary art and music and the decline of Latin as a common language and referring to "sheep-like masses," but he could turn right around and say, "I am not one of these pessimists. I believe that better times are coming." He was devoted to physics and equally engaged with music and violin playing. Likewise, this man of the melancholy visage and world-weary expression also possessed a wicked sense of humor, often pulling pranks on gullible reporters smitten by his image as the inscrutable Sphinx.

And this, of course, brings to mind Einstein's startling public celebrity—a contradiction in and of itself for someone who said, "The cult of individual personalities is always, in my view, unjustified." Reporters, however, were not blessed with Einstein's sense of justification. Though they couldn't take a flying leap at explaining relativity, they were infatuated with the man who propounded the theory. He was pursued as zealously as sports figures and rock stars are today and was asked for his opinion on everything from food to women to, occasionally, science. Though he disliked personal publicity, he, like Garbo, generated it for that very reason. As Otto Friedrich wrote in *Before the Deluge*, "By one of those paradoxes of 20th century publicity, Albert Einstein suddenly became famous precisely because nobody could understand his new theories."

The most important contradiction of this multitudinous man—the true definition of a Renaissance man, is it not?—was between his theoretical work in physics and his view of the human construct known as civilization. He was a relativist in science but not in society. Even the term *relativity* is a misnomer; it should be interpreted, the way Einstein envisaged it, as suggesting the "relationship" of all things. A relativist in ethics wouldn't say, "The fate of the human race is more than ever dependent on its moral strength today," or "The health of society thus depends quite as much on the independence of the individuals composing it as on their close political cohesion."

For someone who was alleged by the press to be so detached from the world, Einstein displayed a keen sense of social responsibility and a very focused and astute idea of what was going on politically. He was an "international" thinker and enlisted the help of world figures who shared his stature—Sigmund Freud, George Bernard Shaw, Bertrand Russell, Upton Sinclair, Charlie Chaplin, Sergei Eisenstein—to raise their voices in support of pacifism and disarmament. He wrote letter after letter encouraging war resistance and denouncing the armaments industry and its feeding into the nationalist fever. He wrote and spoke out on the problems of workers and minorities. He told the world of anti-Semitic atrocities being committed in Germany.

But even Einstein had his limits. As the war clouds in Europe grew darker, and with the fate of his Jewish friends and relations in Germany hanging in the balance, Einstein felt duty bound to warn President Roosevelt of the disturbing scientific news he'd become privy to—the possibility that Hitler might be building an atomic bomb. Soon thereafter, the Manhattan Project was under way in the United States. After the bomb was made and exploded—the scientific know-how for which stemmed from Einstein's early theories of relativity, though not in any way from his personal intervention—Einstein became an even more impassioned spokesman for the scrapping of nuclear weapons programs before they led to an arms race. He lived long enough to learn that the so-called Great Powers were not listening.

One of the final contradictions of Einstein was his unflagging support for an Israeli state. This man who was ambivalent about "nation-states" and who openly despised nationalism was a proponent of Israel from the 1920s, when he first accompanied the famous Zionist Chaim Weizmann on a speaking tour of the United States. As with everything Einstein touched, his explanation of and feelings on this matter were heartfelt and compelling, stemming from his core belief in a God who "is subtle but not malicious" and his Jewishness, for which he could but "thank my lucky stars I belong to the Jewish tradition," which has "an intoxicated joy and amazement at the beauty and grandeur of this world, of which man can just form a faint notion."

After the war, when the move was afoot to establish a state of Israel, Einstein was optimistic about the prospects and the rationale. The Jewish people needed to recover from the psychological trauma they'd undergone, he said, an ordeal that showed the limits of assimilation and thus the need for a solid foundation in a living Jewish society. To those who accused him of promoting nationalism, he deferred that if it were nationalism, "it is a nationalism whose aim is not power but dignity and health." It was so like Einstein to beg for "satisfactory relations" between the Jews and the Arabs in Palestine, calling for "living side by side with our brother the Arab in an open, generous, and worthy manner." And to promote the open dissemination of knowledge that is so vital to a free and generous society, he helped establish The Hebrew University of Jerusalem and Brandeis University in Massachusetts.

Perhaps the sadness we see in the statue of Albert Einstein is at the heart of this latter matter. That is, he saw the possibility of striving for and achieving the ideal—reaching toward the heavens, as it were—but he also had firsthand knowledge of the darker impulses of humankind. With his work in physics, Einstein gave the world a doorway—if not to paradise, then to an improved state of being. He opened the world of the atom for purposes that would make mankind's lot a less painful one. But over the next half century he saw the key he devised in 1905 open one wrong lock after another. By his life's end, photographs show him looking increasingly weighed down by humankind's endless folly, perhaps with some appreciation of his own role in making it possible, if not inevitable. Of his mentor, Jacob Bronowski wrote, "He hated war, and cruelty, and hypocrisy, and above all he hated dogma—except that hate is not the right word for the sense of sad revulsion he felt; he thought hate itself was a kind of dogma."

In 1948, toward the end of his life, Einstein was asked to give an address at Carnegie Hall and accept the pacifist organization One World's first award of merit. Unable to attend because of ill health, he sent someone to read his remarks, which included the following: "We who want peace and the triumph of reason are forced to realize bitterly how diminished is the influence that reason and goodwill exercise today on political events." This no doubt ate at him, coming on the heels of the bomb and the cold war, a climate of cynicism that allowed one of his colleagues to ask Einstein in all seriousness, "Why are you so earnestly opposed to the disappearance of the human race?" In a letter to his wife relating this conversation, Einstein wrote, "I am certain that a century ago nobody could have made such a remark so offhandedly."

■ ■ ■ ■ ■ ■ ■

Albert Einstein did indeed contain multitudes, and the portrait of him contained herein only touches the surface of this remarkable man. His darker ruminations notwithstanding, perhaps it was Einstein's fate to be a bit out of step with his times. This is the fate of all human beings who are—like Galileo, Newton, Lincoln, Gandhi, Whitman—for all times.

THE ALBERT EINSTEIN ARCHIVES

Albert Einstein is undoubtedly one of the most prominent and influential figures of the modern era. As a preeminent physicist, he radically transformed our understanding of the universe. As an ardent humanist, he took an active and outspoken stance on the significant political and social issues of his time. As a committed Jew, he advocated a distinctive moral role for the Jewish people.

Albert Einstein was one of the founders of The Hebrew University of Jerusalem. His unique relationship to this institution found a lasting expression in the bequest of his literary estate and personal papers to The Hebrew University in his Last Will of 1950.

The Jewish National & University Library has been the proud custodian of the Albert Einstein Archives since 1982. This unique cultural asset contains the largest collection of original Einstein manuscripts in the world. It comprises Einstein's vast correspondence with the most influential physicists and intellectuals of the twentieth century.

The Einstein Archives reflects the multifaceted aspects of Albert Einstein's scientific work, political activities, and private life. It provides us with a kaleidoscope—a looking-glass—through which to perceive this great scientist, humanist, and Jew. The bequest of his personal archives was Albert Einstein's most lasting legacy to The Hebrew University. This legacy is both material and spiritual in nature. As heirs to that legacy, it is our responsibility to preserve the archival material, enhance its accessibility, and increase public awareness of the scientific and political activities and the moral and humane values of Albert Einstein.

■ ■ ■ ■ ■ ■ ■

Albert Einstein was not one to retain every piece of paper that passed through his hands. He made no systematic attempt to preserve his papers prior to 1919. As a result of his dramatic rise to fame in November 1919, his correspondence increased vastly. He employed his stepdaughter, Ilse Loewenthal, as his first secretarial assistant, and she achieved the first semblance of well-ordered files. In April 1928, Helen Dukas came to work for Einstein and began to preserve his papers more systematically. Yet not even then were copies of everything kept. Shortly after the Nazis' rise to power in 1933, Einstein's papers were rescued from Berlin by Einstein's son-in-law, Rudolf Kayser, with the help of the French Embassy. The material was brought to Einstein's new home in Princeton and kept there until well after his death. With a few exceptions, the material left at Einstein's summer house in Caputh outside Berlin was destroyed in order to prevent its falling into the hands of Nazi authorities.

Einstein's Will of 1950 appointed his secretary, Helen Dukas, and his close associate Otto Nathan as trustees of his estate. Dukas and Nathan devoted themselves tirelessly for a quarter of a century to organizing the papers and acquiring additional material. As a result of their efforts, the Archives grew threefold. In the 1960s, Helen Dukas and Professor Gerald Holton of Harvard University reorganized the material, thereby rendering it accessible to scholars and preparing it for eventual publication in *The Collected Papers of Albert Einstein*, a joint project of The Hebrew University and Princeton University Press. To facilitate editorial work, the papers were transferred from Einstein's home to the Institute for Advanced Study in Princeton. In 1982, the Einstein Estate transferred all literary rights to The Hebrew University and Einstein's personal papers were transferred to the Jewish National & University Library in Jerusalem. President Avraham Harman and Professor Reuven Yaron of The Hebrew University and Milton Handler of the American Friends of The Hebrew University played a crucial role in securing the transfer of the material to Jerusalem. In 1988 the Bern Dibner Curatorship for the running of the Albert Einstein Archives was established by the Dibner Fund of Connecticut, USA.

Essential
EINSTEIN

OUR TIME IS RICH IN INVENTIVE MINDS, THE INVENTIONS OF WHICH COULD FACILITATE OUR LIVES CONSIDERABLY. We are crossing the seas by power and utilize power also in order to relieve humanity from all tiring muscular work. We have learned to fly and we are able to send messages and news without any difficulty over the entire world through electric waves.

However, the production and distribution of commodities is entirely unorganized so that everybody must live in fear of being eliminated from the economic cycle, in this way suffering for the want of everything. Furthermore, people living in different countries kill each other at irregular time intervals, so that also for this reason anyone who thinks about the future must live in fear and terror. This is due to the fact that the intelligence and character of the masses are incomparably lower than the intelligence and character of the few who produce something valuable for the community.

I trust that posterity will read these statements with a feeling of proud and justified superiority.

—message placed in a time capsule, World's Fair, New York, 1939

A. E. in middle age. Engraving by Rose Weiser. Photographische Gesellschaft, Berlin, n.d. Photograph courtesy AIP Niels Bohr Library

1

THE IDEALS WHICH HAVE LIGHTED MY WAY, AND TIME AFTER TIME HAVE GIVEN ME NEW COURAGE TO FACE life cheerfully, have been Kindness, Beauty, and Truth. Without the sense of kinship with men of like mind, without the occupation with the objective world, the eternally unattainable in the field of art and scientific endeavors, life would have seemed to me empty. The trite objects of human efforts—possessions, outward successes, luxury—have always seemed to me contemptible.

— *"The World as I See It," originally published in* Forum and Century, *1931*

A. E. and his wife, Elsa, Saranac Lake, New York, n.d. Photograph courtesy AIP Niels Bohr Library

MY PASSIONATE SENSE OF SOCIAL JUSTICE AND SOCIAL RESPONSIBILITY HAS ALWAYS CONTRASTED ODDLY WITH my pronounced lack of need for direct contact with other human beings and human communities. I am truly a "lone traveler" and have never belonged to my country, my home, my friends, or even my immediate family with my whole heart. In the face of all these ties I have never lost a sense of distance and a need for solitude—feelings that increase with the years.

—*1930*

A. E. with Elsa and her daughters, Ilse and Margot, c. 1914. Photograph courtesy AIP Niels Bohr Library

5

I MAINTAIN THAT THE COSMIC RELIGIOUS FEELING IS THE STRONGEST AND NOBLEST MOTIVE FOR scientific research. Only those who realize the immense efforts and, above all, the devotion without which pioneer work in theoretical science cannot be achieved are able to grasp the strength of the emotion out of which alone such work, remote as it is from the immediate realities of life, can issue. What a deep conviction of the rationality of the universe and what a yearning to understand, were it but a feeble reflection of the mind revealed in this world, Kepler and Newton must have had to enable them to spend years of solitary labor in disentangling the principles of celestial mechanics! Those whose acquaintance with scientific research is derived chiefly from its practical results easily develop a completely false notion of the mentality of the men who, surrounded by a skeptical world, have shown the way to kindred spirits scattered wide through the world and the centuries. Only one who has devoted his life to similar ends can have a vivid realization of what has inspired these men and given them the strength to remain true to their purpose in spite of countless failures. It is cosmic religious feeling that gives a man such strength. A contemporary has said, not unjustly, that in this materialistic world of ours the serious scientific workers are the only profoundly religious people.

—New York Times Magazine, *1930*

A. E., 1912. Photograph by J. F. Langhans. Photograph courtesy The Hebrew University of Jerusalem, Israel

THE BELIEF IN AN EXTERNAL WORLD INDEPENDENT OF THE PERCEIVING SUBJECT IS THE BASIS OF ALL NATURAL science. Since, however, sense perception only gives information of this external world or of "physical reality" indirectly, we can only grasp the latter by speculative means. It follows from this that our notions of physical reality can never be final.

—on the hundredth anniversary of the birth of Scottish physicist James Clerk Maxwell

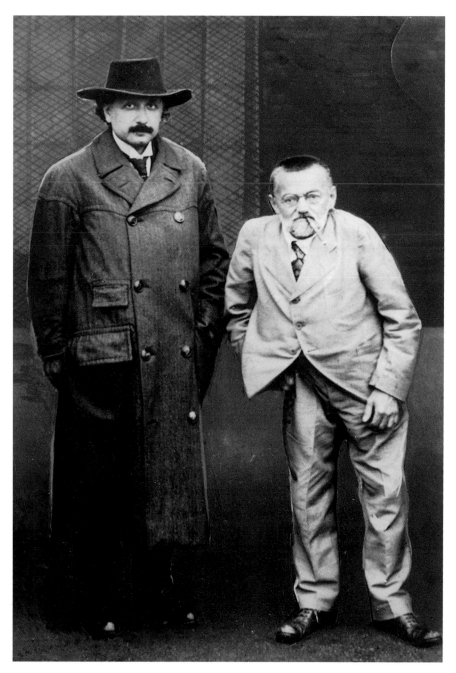

A. E. with American electrical engineer C. P. Steinmetz, c. 1920s. Photograph courtesy Leo Baeck Institute, New York

THE MOST BEAUTIFUL EXPERIENCE WE CAN HAVE IS THE MYSTERIOUS. IT IS THE FUNDAMENTAL EMOTION which stands at the cradle of true art and true science. Whoever does not know it and can no longer wonder, no longer marvel, is as good as dead, and his eyes are dimmed. It was the experience of mystery—even if mixed with fear—that engendered religion. A knowledge of the existence of something we cannot penetrate, our perceptions of the profoundest reason and the most radiant beauty, which only in their most primitive forms are accessible to our minds—it is this knowledge and this emotion that constitute true religiosity; in this sense, and in this alone, I am a deeply religious man.

—*"The World as I See It," originally published in* Forum and Century, *1931*

A. E. in Jerusalem with Elsa, Herbert Samuel, Norman Bentwich, and others, n.d. Photograph courtesy The Hebrew University of Jerusalem, Israel

11

I CANNOT CONCEIVE OF A GOD WHO REWARDS AND PUNISHES HIS CREATURES, OR HAS A WILL OF THE KIND that we experience in ourselves. Neither can I nor would I want to conceive of an individual that survives his physical death; let feeble souls, from fear or absurd egoism, cherish such thoughts. I am satisfied with the mystery of the eternity of life and with the awareness and a glimpse of the marvelous structure of the existing world, together with the devoted striving to comprehend a portion, be it ever so tiny, of the Reason that manifests itself in nature.

— *"The World as I See It," originally published in* Forum and Century, *1931*

A. E., 1935. Photograph courtesy Library of Congress

I AM NOT OF THE OPINION THAT ONE SHOULD MAKE USE OF THE CONCEPT OF GOD IN STRIVING FOR A BETTER world. This, it seems to me, is incompatible with the integrity of a modern cultured person. History shows, moreover, that each party believes, or tries to make others believe, that God is on its side. This makes reasonable understanding and behavior even more difficult. Patient and honest educational work in favor of a moral and enlightened attitude is, in my opinion, the only way to a happier life.

—letter, November 9, 1953

A. E. with Indian poet Rabindranath Tagore, Caputh, Germany, 1930. Photograph courtesy Leo Baeck Institute, New York

15

GREAT SPIRITS HAVE ALWAYS ENCOUNTERED VIOLENT OPPOSITION FROM MEDIOCRE MINDS. THE MEDIOCRE mind is incapable of understanding the man who refuses to bow blindly to conventional prejudices and chooses instead to express his opinions courageously and honestly.

—letter to Morris Raphael Cohen, professor emeritus of philosophy at the College of the City of New York, defending the controversial appointment of Bertrand Russell to a teaching position, March 19, 1940

Photograph courtesy Leo Baeck Institute, New York

THE MORE A MAN IS IMBUED WITH THE ORDERED REGULARITY OF ALL EVENTS THE FIRMER BECOMES HIS conviction that there is no room left by the side of this ordered regularity for causes of a different nature. For him neither the rule of human nor the rule of divine will exists as an independent cause of natural events. To be sure, the doctrine of a personal God interfering with natural events could never be refuted, in the real sense, by science, for this doctrine can always take refuge in those domains in which scientific knowledge has not yet been able to set foot.

—Science, Philosophy and Religion: A Symposium, *1941*

A. E., 1933. Photograph courtesy AIP Niels Bohr Library

SCIENCE CAN ONLY BE CREATED BY THOSE WHO ARE THOROUGHLY IMBUED WITH THE ASPIRATION TOWARD truth and understanding. This source of feeling, however, springs from the sphere of religion. To this there also belongs the faith in the possibility that the regulations valid for the world of existence are rational, that is, comprehensible to reason. I cannot conceive of a genuine scientist without that profound faith. The situation may be expressed by an image: science without religion is lame, religion without science is blind.

—Science, Philosophy and Religion: A Symposium, *1941*

A. E. with Rabindranath Tagore, Berlin. Photograph courtesy The Hebrew University of Jerusalem, Israel

THE EXISTENCE AND VALIDITY OF HUMAN RIGHTS ARE NOT WRITTEN IN THE STARS. THE IDEALS CONCERNING the conduct of men toward each other and the desirable structure of the community have been conceived and taught by enlightened individuals in the course of history. Those ideals and convictions which resulted from historical experience, from the craving for beauty and harmony, have been readily accepted in theory by man—and at all times, have been trampled upon by the same people under the pressure of their animal instincts. A large part of history is therefore replete with the struggle for those human rights, an eternal struggle in which a final victory can never be won. But to tire in that struggle would mean the ruin of society.

—address to the Chicago Decalogue Society, 1954

A. E. and Elsa with Hopi Indians, Grand Canyon, Arizona, n.d. Photograph courtesy The Hebrew University of Jerusalem, Israel

THE PURSUIT OF KNOWLEDGE FOR ITS OWN SAKE, AN ALMOST FANATICAL LOVE OF JUSTICE, AND THE DESIRE for personal independence—these are the features of the Jewish tradition which make me thank my stars that I belong to it.

Those who are raging today against the ideals of reason and individual liberty and are trying to establish a spiritless state-slavery by brute force rightly see in us their irreconcilable foes. History has given us a difficult row to hoe; but so long as we remain devoted servants of truth, justice, and liberty, we shall continue not merely to survive as the oldest of living peoples, but by creative work to bring forth fruits which contribute to the ennoblement of the human race, as heretofore.

—Mein Weltbild, *1934*

A. E. in Berlin, December 1932. Photograph by Charles Holdt, courtesy AIP Niels Bohr Library

FULFILLMENT ON THE MORAL AND ESTHETIC SIDE IS A GOAL WHICH LIES CLOSER TO THE PREOCCUPATIONS OF art than it does to those of science. Of course, understanding of our fellow-beings is important. But this understanding becomes fruitful only when it is sustained by sympathetic feeling in joy and in sorrow. The cultivation of this most important spring of moral action is that which is left of religion when it has been purified of the elements of superstition. In this sense, religion forms an important part of education, where it receives far too little consideration, and that little not sufficiently systematic.

The frightful dilemma of the political world situation has much to do with this sin of omission on the part of our civilization. Without this "ethical culture" there is no salvation for humanity.

—on the seventy-fifth anniversary of the Ethical Culture Society, New York, 1951

A. E. and Elsa en route to the United States on the SS Rotterdam, 1921. Photograph courtesy AIP Niels Bohr Library

NOTHING TRULY VALUABLE CAN BE ACHIEVED EXCEPT BY THE DISINTERESTED COOPERATION OF MANY individuals. Hence the man of good will is never happier than when some communal enterprise is afoot and is launched at the cost of heavy sacrifices, with the single object of promoting life and culture.

—address preceding a lecture on physics given at a resort for tubercular patients, Switzerland, 1928

A. E. with Austrian physicist Paul Ehrenfest and Dutch astronomer Willem de Sitter (back row) and English astronomer Arthur Eddington and Dutch physicist Hendrik Lorentz (front row), Leiden, Netherlands. Photograph courtesy Leo Baeck Institute, New York

WHERE THE WORLD CEASES TO BE THE SCENE OF OUR PERSONAL HOPES AND WISHES, WHERE WE FACE IT AS free beings admiring, asking, and observing, there we enter the realm of Art and Science. If what is seen and experienced is portrayed in the language of logic, we are engaged in science. If it is communicated through forms whose connections are not accessible to the conscious mind but are recognized intuitively as meaningful, then we are engaged in art. Common to both is the loving devotion to that which transcends personal concerns and volition.

—*letter to the editor of a German magazine regarding the connection between art and science in any epoch, 1927*

A. E., Pasadena, California, c. 1930. Photograph courtesy The Hebrew University of Jerusalem, Israel

I T IS THROUGH THEIR SCIENTIFIC CONTRIBUTIONS AND ARTISTIC ACHIEVEMENTS THAT INTELLECTUALS CAN do most to advance international reconciliation and the brotherhood of man. Creative work lifts man above personal and selfish national goals. To concentrate on the problems and aspirations which all thinking men share creates a sense of comradeship that is eventually bound to reunite scholars and artists of all nations; it is unavoidable that, at times, political passions will divide those among them who are less broad-minded and lack the ability to think independently. Intellectuals should never tire of emphasizing the international character of mankind's cherished heritage. They must never allow themselves to be exploited in the service of political passions in their public declarations or any other public activity.

*—contribution to a memorial volume for the German Club for the
Cultivation of Social and Scientific Relations, New York, 1920*

Photograph courtesy Leo Baeck Institute, New York

THERE EXISTS A PASSION FOR COMPREHENSION, JUST AS THERE EXISTS A PASSION FOR MUSIC. THAT PASSION is rather common in children, but gets lost in most people later on. Without this passion, there would be neither mathematics nor natural science. Time and again the passion for understanding has led to the illusion that man is able to comprehend the objective world rationally, by pure thought, without any empirical foundations—in short, by metaphysics. I believe that every true theorist is a kind of tamed metaphysicist, no matter how pure a "positivist" he may fancy himself. The metaphysicist believes that the logically simple is also the real. The tamed metaphysicist believes that not all that is logically simple is embodied in experienced reality, but that the totality of all sensory experience can be "comprehended" on the basis of a conceptual system built on premises of great simplicity. The skeptic will say that this is a "miracle creed." Admittedly so, but it is a miracle creed which has been borne out to an amazing extent by the development of science.

—Scientific American, *1950*

34

Photograph courtesy Leo Baeck Institute, New York

THE TRUE VALUE OF A HUMAN BEING IS DETERMINED PRIMARILY BY THE MEASURE AND THE SENSE IN WHICH he has attained liberation from the self.

—Mein Weltbild, *1934*

A. E. at the home of Ben Meyer, trustee of the California Institute of Technology, near Santa Barbara, February 1933. Photograph courtesy California Institute of Technology Archives

As for the search for truth, I know from my own painful searching, with its many blind alleys, how hard it is to take a reliable step, be it ever so small, toward the understanding of that which is truly significant.

—letter, February 1934

Photograph courtesy Leo Baeck Institute, New York

THERE ARE ONLY A FEW ENLIGHTENED PEOPLE WITH A LUCID MIND AND STYLE AND WITH GOOD TASTE WITHIN a century. What has been preserved of their work belongs among the most precious possessions of mankind. We owe it to a few writers of antiquity that the people of the Middle Ages could slowly extricate themselves from the superstitions and ignorance that had darkened life for more than half a millennium.

Nothing is more needed to overcome the modernist's snobbishness.

—Jungkaufmann, *1952*

A. E. with C. E. St. John, looking at solar spectrum, Mount Wilson Observatory, Pasadena, California, 1931.
Photograph by Ferdinand Ellerman, courtesy Leo Baeck Institute, New York

MAN IS, AT ONE AND THE SAME TIME, A SOLITARY BEING AND A SOCIAL BEING. AS A SOLITARY BEING, HE attempts to protect his own existence and that of those who are closest to him, to satisfy his personal desires, and to develop his innate abilities. As a social being, he seeks to gain the recognition and affection of his fellow human beings, to share in their pleasures, to comfort them in their sorrows, and to improve their conditions of life. Only the existence of these varied, frequently conflicting strivings accounts for the special character of a man, and their specific combination determines the extent to which an individual can achieve an inner equilibrium and can contribute to the well-being of society.

—Monthly Review, *1949*

A. E., n.d. Photograph courtesy Library of Congress

I COULD SING A HYMN OF PRAISE ABOUT THE PROGRESS MADE IN THE FIELD OF APPLIED SCIENCE; AND NO doubt, you yourselves will promote further progress during your lifetime. I could speak in such terms since this is the century of applied science, and America is its fatherland. But I do not want to use such language. . . . Why does applied science, which is so magnificent, saves work and makes life easier, bring us so little happiness? The simple answer is that we have not yet learned to make proper use of it.

—*address at the California Institute of Technology, 1931*

A. E. with German chemist Fritz Haber, n.d. Photograph courtesy AIP Niels Bohr Library

DO NOT PRIDE YOURSELF ON THE FEW GREAT MEN WHO, OVER THE CENTURIES, HAVE BEEN BORN ON YOUR earth—through no merit of yours. Reflect, rather, on how you treated them at the time, and how you have followed their teachings.

—n.d.

A. E. (seated, far left) with the graduating class of the cantonal school, Aarau, Switzerland, 1896. Photograph courtesy Leo Baeck Institute, New York

FOR MYSELF, THE STRUGGLE TO GAIN MORE INSIGHT AND UNDERSTANDING IS ONE OF THOSE INDEPENDENT objectives without which a thinking individual would find it impossible to have a conscious, positive attitude toward life.

It is the very essence of our striving for understanding that, on the one hand, it attempts to encompass the great and complex variety of man's experience, and that on the other, it looks for simplicity and economy in the basic assumptions. The belief that these two objectives can exist side by side is, in view of the primitive state of our scientific knowledge, a matter of faith. Without such faith I could not have a strong and unshakable conviction about the independent value of knowledge.

—*message to the Italian Society for the Advancement of Science, Lucca, Italy, 1950*

A. E., n.d. Photograph courtesy AIP Niels Bohr Library, Dorothy Davis Locanthi Collection

KNOWLEDGE EXISTS IN TWO FORMS—LIFELESS, STORED IN BOOKS, AND ALIVE IN THE CONSCIOUSNESS OF MEN. The second form of existence is after all the essential one; the first, indispensable as it may be, occupies only an inferior position.

—*message to the Morris Raphael Cohen Student Memorial Fund, 1949*

A. E. at home in Caputh, Germany, c. 1931. Photograph courtesy The Hebrew University of Jerusalem, Israel

MAN TRIES TO MAKE FOR HIMSELF IN THE FASHION THAT SUITS HIM BEST A SIMPLIFIED AND INTELLIGIBLE picture of the world; he then tries to some extent to substitute this cosmos of his for the world of experience, and thus to overcome it. This is what the painter, the poet, the speculative philosopher, and the natural scientist do, each in his own fashion. Each makes this cosmos and its construction the pivot of his emotional life, in order to find in this way the peace and security which he cannot find in the narrow whirlpool of personal experience.

—address to the Physical Society at a celebration of Max Planck's sixtieth birthday, Berlin, 1918

A. E. with Z. Gezari in A. E.'s backyard, Princeton, New Jersey, May 1954. Photograph courtesy AIP Niels Bohr Library

53

It is best, it seems to me, to separate one's inner striving from one's trade as far as possible. It is not good when one's daily bread is tied to God's special blessing.

—letter, May 18, 1950

A. E. and Elsa in Palm Springs, California. Photograph courtesy Leo Baeck Institute, New York

THE SCHOOL OF LIFE IS UNPLANNED AND CHAOTIC WHILE THE EDUCATIONAL SYSTEM OPERATES ACCORDING to a definite scheme. . . . That explains . . . why education is such an important political instrument: there is always the danger that it may become an object of exploitation by contending political groups. While at school, the student may be taught ominous prejudices from which he may find it difficult to free himself in later years. The process of education may be so controlled by the state that its citizens will be kept in intellectual bondage.

—*message to the New Jersey Education Association, Atlantic City, 1939*

A. E. sailing, 1936. Photograph courtesy AIP Niels Bohr Library

O Youth: DO YOU KNOW THAT YOURS IS NOT THE FIRST GENERATION TO YEARN FOR A LIFE FULL OF BEAUTY and freedom? Do you know that all your ancestors felt as you do—and fell victim to trouble and hatred?

Do you know, also, that your fervent wishes can only find fulfillment if you succeed in attaining love and understanding of men, and animals, and plants, and stars, so that every joy becomes your joy and every pain your pain? Open your eyes, your heart, your hands, and avoid the poison your forebears so greedily sucked in from History. Then will all the earth be your fatherland, and all your work and effort spread forth blessings.

—inscription in an album for a neighbor's daughter, Caputh, Germany, 1932

A. E. with baby John Steidig, Deep Creek Lake, Maryland, c. 1946. Photograph by Ruhl Studios, courtesy The Hebrew University of Jerusalem, Israel

BEAR IN MIND THAT THE WONDERFUL THINGS YOU LEARN IN YOUR SCHOOLS ARE THE WORK OF MANY generations, produced by enthusiastic effort and infinite labor in every country of the world. All this is put into your hands as your inheritance in order that you may receive it, honor it, add to it, and one day faithfully hand it to your children. Thus do we mortals achieve immortality in the permanent things which we create in common.

—address to a group of children, 1934

D. H. Menzel, A. E., American mathematician George Birkhoff, and American astronomer Harlow Shapley's son, Carl,
at the time of Einstein's receiving an honorary degree from Harvard University, Cambridge, Massachusetts, 1935.
Photograph courtesy AIP Niels Bohr Library

IT IS NOT ENOUGH TO TEACH MAN A SPECIALTY. THROUGH IT HE MAY BECOME A KIND OF USEFUL MACHINE BUT not a harmoniously developed personality. It is essential that the student acquire an understanding of and a lively feeling for values. He must acquire a vivid sense of the beautiful and of the morally good. Otherwise he—with his specialized knowledge—more closely resembles a well-trained dog than a harmoniously developed person. He must learn to understand the motives of human beings, their illusions, and their sufferings in order to acquire a proper relationship to individual fellow-men and to the community.

These precious things are conveyed through personal contact with those who teach, not—or at least not in the main—through textbooks. It is this that primarily constitutes and preserves culture. This is what I have in mind when I recommend the "humanities" as important, not just dry specialized knowledge in the fields of history and philosophy.

Overemphasis on the competitive system and premature specialization on the ground of immediate usefulness kill the spirit on which all cultural life depends, specialized knowledge included.

—New York Times, *1952*

A. E., c. 1950. Photograph courtesy The Hebrew University of Jerusalem, Israel

THE SCHOOL HAS ALWAYS BEEN THE MOST IMPORTANT MEANS OF TRANSFERRING THE WEALTH OF TRADITION from one generation to the next. This applies today in an even higher degree than in former times, for through modern development of the economic life, the family as bearer of tradition and education has been weakened. The continuance and health of human society is therefore in a still higher degree dependent on the school than formerly.

—address at a celebration of the tercentenary of higher education in America, Albany, New York, 1936

Photograph courtesy Leo Baeck Institute, New York

I AM ABSOLUTELY CONVINCED THAT NO WEALTH IN THE WORLD CAN HELP HUMANITY FORWARD, EVEN IN the hands of the most devoted worker in this cause. The example of great and pure individuals is the only thing that can lead us to noble thoughts and deeds. Money only appeals to selfishness and irresistibly invites abuse.

Can anyone imagine Moses, Jesus, or Gandhi armed with the money-bags of Carnegie?

—Mein Weltbild, *1934*

A. E. in Caputh, Germany, October 1929. Photograph courtesy Leo Baeck Institute, New York

My political ideal is democracy. Let every man be respected as an individual and no man idolized. It is an irony of fate that I myself have been the recipient of excessive admiration and reverence from my fellow-beings, through no fault, and no merit, of my own. The cause of this may well be the desire, unattainable for many, to understand the few ideas to which I have with my own feeble powers attained through ceaseless struggle. I am quite aware that it is necessary for the achievement of the objective of an organization that one man should do the thinking and directing and generally bear the responsibility. But the led must not be coerced, they must be able to choose their leader. An autocratic system of coercion, in my opinion, soon degenerates. For force always attracts men of low morality, and I believe it to be an invariable rule that tyrants of genius are succeeded by scoundrels.

— *"The World as I See It," originally published in* Forum and Century, *1931*

A. E., Leiden, Netherlands, 1923. Photograph by Gerhard H. Dieke,
courtesy AIP Niels Bohr Library

WHAT CAN THE SCHOOLS DO TO DEFEND DEMOCRACY? SHOULD THEY PREACH A SPECIFIC POLITICAL DOCTRINE? I believe they should not. If they are able to teach young people to have a critical mind and a socially oriented attitude, they will have done all that is necessary. Students will then become equipped with those qualities which are prerequisite for citizens living in a healthy democratic society.

—message to the New Jersey Education Association, Atlantic City, 1939

A. E.'s secretary, Helen Dukas, A. E., and Margot Einstein taking the U.S. oath of allegiance, 1940.
Photograph courtesy AIP Niels Bohr Library

DEMOCRACY, TAKEN IN ITS NARROWER, PURELY POLITICAL, SENSE SUFFERS FROM THE FACT THAT THOSE IN economic and political power possess the means for molding public opinion to serve their own class interests. The democratic form of government in itself does not automatically solve problems; it offers, however, a useful framework for their solution. Everything depends ultimately on the political and moral qualities of the citizenry.

—*interview in the* Cheyney Record, *student newspaper of Cheyney State Teachers College, Cheyney, Pennsylvania, 1948*

Photograph courtesy Leo Baeck Institute, New York

I REGARD IT AS THE CHIEF DUTY OF THE STATE TO PROTECT THE INDIVIDUAL AND GIVE HIM THE OPPORTUNITY to develop into a creative personality.

That is to say, the state should be our servant and not we its slaves. The state transgresses this commandment when it compels us by force to engage in military and war service, the more so since the object and the effect of this slavish service is to kill people belonging to other countries or interfere with their freedom of development. We are only to make such sacrifices to the state as will promote the free development of individual human beings.

—The Nation, *1931*

A. E., c. 1930. Photograph courtesy AIP Niels Bohr Library

SMALL IS THE NUMBER OF THEM THAT SEE WITH THEIR OWN EYES AND FEEL WITH THEIR OWN HEARTS. BUT it is their strength that will decide whether the human race must relapse into that state of stupor which a deluded multitude appears today to regard as the ideal.

O that the nations might see, before it is too late, how much of their self-determination they have got to sacrifice in order to avoid the struggle of all against all!

The power of conscience and of the international spirit has proved itself inadequate. At present it is being so weak as to tolerate parleying with the worst enemies of civilization. There is a kind of compliance which is a crime against humanity, though it passes for political wisdom.

—Mein Weltbild, *1934*

A. E. with King Albert of Belgium, Laeken, 1933. Photograph by Queen Elisabeth of Belgium, courtesy The Hebrew University of Jerusalem, Israel

DARWIN'S THEORY OF THE STRUGGLE FOR EXISTENCE AND THE SELECTIVITY CONNECTED WITH IT HAS BY many people been cited as authorization of the encouragement of the spirit of competition. Some people also in such a way have tried to prove pseudoscientifically the necessity of the destructive economic struggle of competition between individuals. But this is wrong, because man owes his strength in the struggle for existence to the fact that he is a socially living animal. As little as a battle between single ants on an ant hill is essential for survival, just so little is this the case with the individual members of a human community.

—address at a celebration of the tercentenary of higher education in America, Albany, New York, 1936

A. E. and Elsa with others at a tea ceremony, Japan, 1922. Photograph courtesy Leo Baeck Institute, New York

Anti-Semitism has always been the cheapest means employed by selfish minorities for deceiving the people. A tyranny based on such deception and maintained by terror must inevitably perish from the poison it generates within itself. For the pressure of accumulated injustice strengthens those moral forces in man which lead to a liberation and purification of public life. May our community through its suffering and its work contribute toward the release of those liberating forces.

—address to the National Labor Committee for Palestine, New York, 1938

A. E., n.d. Photograph courtesy AIP Niels Bohr Library

WHAT IS THE MEANING OF HUMAN LIFE, OR, FOR THAT MATTER, OF THE LIFE OF ANY CREATURE? TO KNOW AN answer to this question means to be religious. You ask: Does it make any sense, then, to pose this question? I answer: The man who regards his own life and that of his fellow creatures as meaningless is not merely unhappy but hardly fit for life.

—Mein Weltbild, *1934*

A. E. and Elsa aboard the Kitano Maru. *Photograph courtesy The Hebrew University of Jerusalem, Israel*

YOU ASK ME WHAT I THINK ABOUT WAR AND THE DEATH PENALTY. THE LATTER IS SIMPLER. I AM NOT FOR punishment all, but only for measures that serve society and its protection. In principle I would not be opposed to killing individuals who are worthless or dangerous in that sense. I am against it only because I do not trust people, i.e. the courts. What I value in life is quality rather than quantity, just as in Nature the overall principles represent a higher reality than does a single object.

—letter, November 4, 1931

A. E. and Marie Curie walking near Lake Geneva after a meeting of the International Committee on Intellectual Cooperation, c. 1930.
Photograph courtesy AIP Niels Bohr Library

WHAT NEED IS THERE FOR A CRITERION OF RESPONSIBILITY? I BELIEVE THAT THE HORRIFYING DETERIORATION in the ethical conduct of people today stems primarily from the mechanization and dehumanization of our lives—a disastrous byproduct of the development of the scientific and technical mentality. Nostra culpa! I don't see any way to tackle this disastrous short-coming. Man grows cold faster than the planet he inhabits.

—letter to Dr. Otto Juliusburger, April 11, 1946

Photograph courtesy Leo Baeck Institute, New York

WHOEVER UNDERTAKES TO SET HIMSELF UP AS JUDGE IN THE FIELD OF TRUTH AND KNOWLEDGE IS shipwrecked by the laughter of the gods.

—contribution to a publication commemorating the eightieth birthday of German rabbi and theologian Leo Baeck, 1953

Photograph courtesy Leo Baeck Institute, New York

Taken on the whole, I would believe that Gandhi's views were the most enlightened of all the political men in our time. We should strive to do things in his spirit . . . not to use violence in fighting for our cause, but by non-participation in what we believe is evil.

—*United Nations radio interview recorded in Einstein's study, Princeton, New Jersey, 1950*

Photograph courtesy Leo Baeck Institute, New York

I DO NOT CONSIDER MYSELF THE FATHER OF THE RELEASE OF ATOMIC ENERGY. MY PART IN IT WAS QUITE indirect. I did not, in fact, foresee that it would be released in my time. I believed only that it was theoretically possible. It became practical through the accidental discovery of chain reaction, and this was not something I could have predicted.

—Atlantic Monthly, *1945*

A. E., n.d. Photograph courtesy Library of Congress

THE DISCOVERY OF NUCLEAR CHAIN REACTIONS NEED NOT BRING ABOUT THE DESTRUCTION OF MANKIND, ANY more than did the discovery of matches. We only must do everything in our power to safeguard against its abuse. In the present stage of technical development, only a supranational organization, equipped with a sufficiently strong executive power, can protect us. Once we have understood that, we shall find the strength for the sacrifices necessary to ensure the future of mankind. Each one of us would be at fault if the goal were not reached in time. There is the danger that everyone waits idly for others to act in his stead.

—*message for Canadian Education Week, March 2–8, 1952*

Photograph courtesy Leo Baeck Institute, New York

WE SCIENTISTS, WHOSE TRAGIC DESTINATION HAS BEEN TO HELP IN MAKING THE METHODS OF ANNIHILATION more gruesome and more effective, must consider it our solemn and transcendent duty to do all in our power in preventing these weapons from being used for the brutal purpose for which they were invented. What task could possibly be more important to us? What social aim could be closer to our hearts?

—undelivered message to the Peace Congress of Intellectuals, Wroclav, Poland, released to the press, 1948

A. E. with Yeshiva University officials Samuel Belkin and Michael Nisselson (at far right, New York Times *editor Benjamin Fine), arranging for the naming of Albert Einstein College of Medicine. Photograph courtesy AIP Niels Bohr Library*

ANYBODY WHO REALLY WANTS TO ABOLISH WAR MUST RESOLUTELY DECLARE HIMSELF IN FAVOR OF HIS OWN country's resigning a portion of its sovereignty in favor of international institutions: he must be ready to make his own country amenable, in case of a dispute, to the award of an international court. He must, in the most uncompromising fashion, support disarmament all round, as is actually envisaged in the unfortunate Treaty of Versailles; unless military and aggressively patriotic education is abolished, we can hope for no progress.

—Mein Weltbild, *1934*

A. E. in his study, Princeton, New Jersey, c. 1946. Photograph courtesy The Hebrew University of Jerusalem, Israel

WAR CONSTITUTES THE MOST FORMIDABLE OBSTACLE TO THE GROWTH OF INTERNATIONAL COOPERATION, especially in its effect upon culture. War destroys all those conditions which are indispensable to the intellectual if he is to work creatively. If he happens to be young and vigorous, his energies will be chained to the engines of destruction, while older men will be trapped in an atmosphere of hate and frustration. Moreover, war leads to the impoverishment of nations and to long periods of economic depression. Hence, he who cherishes the values of culture cannot fail to be a pacifist.

—*article contributed to* Die Friedensbewegung, *German handbook of the pacifist movement, 1922*

A. E. with American physicist Wolfgang Pauli, 1926. Photograph courtesy CERN, AIP Niels Bohr Library

THE DESTINY OF CIVILIZED HUMANITY DEPENDS MORE THAN EVER ON THE MORAL FORCES IT IS CAPABLE OF generating. Hence the task that confronts our age is certainly no easier than the tasks our immediate predecessors successfully performed. . . . The way to a joyful and happy existence is everywhere through self-limitation.

Where can the strength for such a process come from? Only from those who have had the chance in their early years to fortify their minds and broaden their outlook through study. Thus we of the older generation look to you and hope that you will strive with all your might and achieve what was denied to us.

—address to German pacifist students, c. 1930

A. E. and Elsa with students at an unidentified school, n.d.

THE REALLY VALUABLE THING IN THE PAGEANT OF HUMAN LIFE SEEMS TO ME NOT THE POLITICAL STATE, but the creative, sentient individual, the personality; it alone creates the noble and the sublime, while the herd as such remains dull in thought and dull in feeling.

This topic brings me to that worst outcrop of herd life, the military system, which I abhor. That a man can take pleasure in marching in fours to the strains of a band is enough to make me despise him. He has only been given his big brain by mistake; unprotected spinal marrow was all he needed. This plague-spot of civilization ought to be abolished with all possible speed. Heroism on command, senseless violence, and all the loathsome nonsense that goes by the name of patriotism—how passionately I hate them! How vile and despicable seems war to me!

— *"The World as I See It," originally published in* Forum and Century, *1931*

A. E., Princeton, New Jersey, May 1954. Photograph courtesy AIP Niels Bohr Library, Gezari Collection

THE MAN OF SCIENCE, AS WE CAN OBSERVE WITH OUR OWN EYES, SUFFERS A TRULY TRAGIC FATE. STRIVING in great sincerity for clarity and inner independence, he himself, through his sheer super-human efforts, has fashioned the tools which are being used to make him a slave and to destroy him also from within. He cannot escape being muzzled by those who have the political power in their hands. As a soldier he is forced to sacrifice his own life and to destroy the lives of others even when he is convinced of the absurdity of such sacrifices. He is fully aware of the fact that universal destruction is unavoidable since the historical development has led to the concentration of all economic, political, and military power in the hands of the national states. He also realizes that mankind can be saved only if a supranational system, based on law, would be created to eliminate for good the methods of brute force. However, the man of science has slipped so much that he accepts the slavery inflicted upon him by national states as his inevitable fate. He even degrades himself to such an extent that he helps obediently in the perfection of the means for the general destruction of mankind.

—*message to the Italian Society for the Advancement of Science, Lucca, Italy, 1950*

A. E. with American physicist J. R. Oppenheimer at the Institute for Advanced Study, 1947. Photograph courtesy AIP Niels Bohr Library

THE DEVELOPMENT OF TECHNOLOGY, RESULTING FROM THE WORK OF SCIENTISTS, HAS MADE THE ECONOMIES of the world interdependent: this is why every war must assume world-wide importance. Only when we come to appreciate the significance of this development shall we be able to muster the energy and good will needed to create an organization that will make war impossible.

—*article contributed to* Die Friedensbewegung, *German handbook of the pacifist movement, 1922*

Dutch physicist Peter Zeeman, A. E., and Austrian physicist Paul Ehrenfest in Zeeman's laboratory, Amsterdam, n.d.
Photograph courtesy AIP Niels Bohr Library

HOW DOES ONE ACTIVATE PEOPLE WHO ARE TIRED, HARASSED AND ALSO LAZY? IT IS LIKE THE FOUNDING of a new religion. It almost never succeeds, and if it does succeed, one is at a loss to know why.

The people who are leading us to destruction sometimes make speeches which reveal quite clearly that they do not lack the proper insight. In the final analysis, however, every man acts according to the pressure of his personal situation and in his own interests.

I myself express openly what I think. But I know that does not mean that I could create a popular movement such as Gandhi was able to do. You can be sure that nothing can be achieved solely by preaching reason.

—letter, 1954

A. E. and Danish physicist Niels Bohr, n.d. Photograph by Paul Ehrenfest, courtesy AIP Niels Bohr Library

So far as we, the physicists, are concerned, we are no politicians and it has never been our wish to meddle in politics. But we know a few things that the politicians do not know. And we feel the duty to speak up and to remind those responsible that there is no escape into easy comforts, there is no distance ahead for proceeding little by little and delaying the necessary changes into an indefinite future, there is no time left for petty bargaining. The situation calls for a courageous effort, for a radical change in our whole attitude, in the entire political concept. May the spirit that prompted Alfred Nobel to create his great institution, the spirit of trust and confidence, of generosity and brotherhood among men, prevail in the minds of those upon whose decisions our destiny rests. Otherwise, human civilization is doomed.

—*address at the Fifth Nobel Anniversary Dinner, New York, 1945*

A. E., c. 1930. Photograph by John Hagemeyer, courtesy AIP Niels Bohr Library

WE SHOULD BE ON OUR GUARD NOT TO OVERESTIMATE SCIENCE AND SCIENTIFIC METHODS WHEN IT IS A question of human problems; and we should not assume that experts are the only ones who have the right to express themselves on questions affecting the organization of society.

—Monthly Review, *1949*

A. E. with C. E. St. John, staff member of Mount Wilson Observatory, c. 1931. Photograph courtesy Library of Congress

Previous generations were able to look upon intellectual and cultural progress as simply the inherited fruits of their forebears' labors, which made life easier and more beautiful for them. But the calamities of our times show us that this was a fatal illusion.

We see now that the greatest efforts are needed if this legacy of humanity's is to prove a blessing and not a curse. For whereas formerly it was enough for a man to have freed himself to some extent from personal egotism to make him a valuable member of society, today he must also be required to overcome national and class egotism. Only if he reaches those heights can he contribute toward improving the lot of humanity.

—Mein Weltbild, *1934*

A. E. and Niels Bohr in conversation at the home of Paul Ehrenfest. Photograph by Paul Ehrenfest, courtesy AIP
Niels Bohr Library

WHAT HOPES AND FEARS DOES THE SCIENTIFIC METHOD IMPLY FOR MANKIND? I DO NOT THINK THAT THIS is the right way to put the question. Whatever this tool in the hand of man will produce depends entirely on the nature of the goals alive in this mankind. Once these goals exist, the scientific method furnishes means to realize them. Yet it cannot furnish the very goals. The scientific method itself would not have led anywhere, it would not even have been born without a passionate striving for clear understanding.

Perfection of means and confusion of goals seem—in my opinion—to characterize our age. If we desire sincerely and passionately the safety, the welfare, and the free development of the talents of all men, we shall not be in want of the means to approach such a state. Even if only a small part of mankind strives for such goals, their superiority will prove itself in the long run.

—broadcast recording for Science Conference, London, 1941

A. E., Pasadena, California, 1932. Photograph courtesy AIP Niels Bohr Library

Select Bibliography of Einstein's Writings

Essays on Science. New York: Philosophical Library, 1934.

The Evolution of Physics (with L. Infeld). Cambridge: Cambridge University Press, 1947.

Ideas and Opinions. New York: Crown, 1954; Dell, 1973.

The Meaning of Relativity. Princeton: Princeton University Press, 1950.

Out of My Later Years. New York: Philosophical Library, 1950.

The Principle of Relativity (with H. A. Lorentz, H. Minkowski, and H. Weyl). New York: Dover, 1952.

Relativity: The Special and General Theory. New York: Crown, 1961.

The World As I See It. London: John Lane, 1935.

Suggested Readings

Carter, Nigel. *Einstein's Universe.* New York: Viking Press, 1979.

Clark, Ronald W. *Einstein: The Life and Times. An Illustrated Biography.* New York: Abrams, 1984.

Dukas, Helen, and Banesh Hoffman, eds. *Albert Einstein: The Human Side.* Princeton, N.J.: Princeton University Press, 1979.

French, A. P., ed. *Einstein: A Centenary Volume.* Cambridge: Harvard University Press, 1979.

Hoffman, Banesh, and Helen Dukas. *Albert Einstein: Creator and Rebel.* New York: Viking Press, 1972.

Holton, Gerald, and Yehuda Elkana, eds. *Albert Einstein: Historical and Cultural Perspectives. The Centennial Symposium in Jerusalem.* Princeton, N.J.: Princeton University Press, 1982.

Pais, Abraham. *Subtle Is the Lord: The Science and Life of Albert Einstein.* Oxford and New York: Oxford University Press, 1982.

Richards, Alan Windsor. *Einstein As I Knew Him.* Princeton, N.J.: Harvest House Press, 1979.